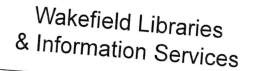

Wakefield Libraries
& Information Services

book should be returned by the last date stamped
e. You may renew the loan personally, by post or
ne for a further period if the book is not required by
another reader.

’s

To Bill Hamilton

Jesus' Day Off

A RED FOX BOOK 978 0 099 26273 2

First published in Great Britain by Hutchinson,
an imprint of Random House Children's Publishers UK

Hutchinson edition published 1998
Red Fox edition published 2002

10

Red Fox Books are published by Random House Children's Publishers UK,
61–63 Uxbridge Road, London W5 5SA,
a division of The Random House Group Ltd,
Addresses for companies within The Random
House Group Limited can be found at:
www.randomhouse.co.uk/offices.htm

THE RANDOM HOUSE GROUP Limited Reg. No. 954009
www.randomhousechildrens.co.uk

A CIP catalogue record for this book is available from the British Library.

Printed in Singapore by Tien Wah Press

This is Jesus.

Bartholomew Andrew Philip Simon Judas Matthe

These are his friends.

Peter   Thomas   Judas   John   James   James
                   Iscariot

He had twelve of them.

Jesus could do amazing miracles,
and no one could work out
how they were done.

He also told
marvellous stories,
all for free.

Each day he worked hard to make

everything around him beautiful . . .

... until one day he woke up exhausted from saving the world.

That day
the miracles
didn't go quite
so well . . .

. . . nor
did the stories.

The next morning Jesus went to the doctor.

After examining him the doctor advised,
'Take the day off, Jesus. Relax. Enjoy yourself.
Sit in the sun.'

So Jesus told his friends what the doctor
had ordered, and then went out for a walk.
It was a lovely cloudless day.

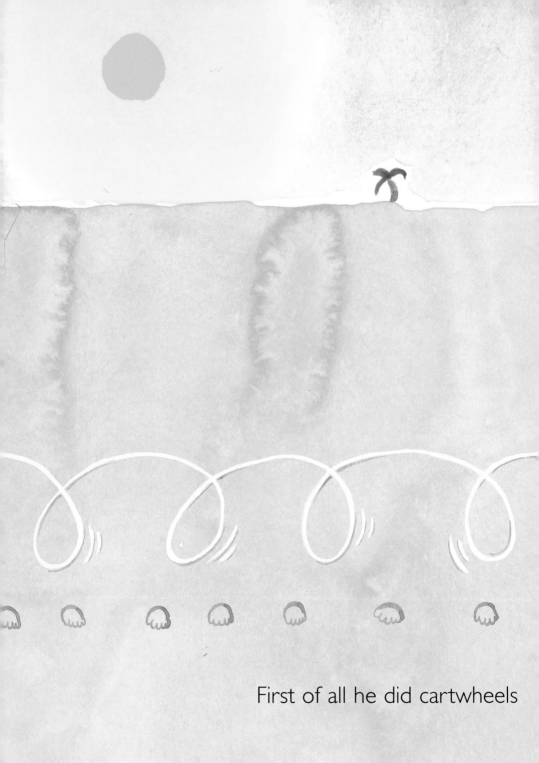

First of all he did cartwheels

right across the desert.

Then he played catch with his halo.

Then he had a picnic.

After that he had a refreshing swim.

And finally he went on a long donkey ride —
something he always enjoyed.

It had been a wonderful day. But towards the
end, as he sat in the sun, Jesus suddenly felt sad.
For really the day had been wasted, and he'd
helped no one.

In fact, he felt so bad he decided to tell
his dad all about it.

Jesus loved his dad
very much. Dad knew
everything, and always
had the right thing
to say.

When Jesus told him about his day off,
his dad said, 'Look down there a minute, son.'
So Jesus looked down.

'Where you did your cartwheels, fountains of water appeared in the desert...

...where you threw your halo and ate your picnic, the trees bloomed with fruit...

...when you went swimming, the fishermen had lots of luck...

...and whoever you passed on your donkey, felt instantly happy.'

'So you see, when you're feeling better yourself, you can only make others feel better too.'

Jesus knew that, as usual, his father was right.

'Thanks, dad,' he said.

When Jesus got home his friends were
so happy to see him looking so well, they
cooked him a delicious supper.

That night, after he'd said his prayers, Jesus
slept soundly.

The next morning he was glad he'd taken a rest. He had this funny feeling there was a *lot* more good work to be done.

The end

THE GREATEST ADVENTURES IN THE WORLD

William Tell
AND THE
APPLE FOR FREEDOM

TONY BRADMAN & TONY ROSS

ORCHARD

ORCHARD BOOKS

The text was first published in Great Britain in a gift collection called
The Orchard Book of Swords, Sorcerers and Superheroes with full colour illustrations by
Tony Ross, in 2003
This edition first published in hardback in 2004
First paperback publication in 2005

3 5 7 9 10 8 6 4 2

A CIP catalogue record for this book is available from the British Library.

ISBN 978 1 84362 476 9

Printed and bound in Germany by GGP Media GmbH, Poessneck

The paper and board used in this book are made from wood from responsible sources

Orchard Books
An imprint of Hachette Children's Group
Part of The Watts Publishing Group Limited
Carmelite House, 50 Victoria Embankment, London EC4Y 0DZ

An Hachette UK Company
www.hachette.co.uk
www.hachettechildrens.co.uk